My Family Tree in Palestine

in

Richard M. Dudum

SAN FRANCISCO

Thank you, Randa.

Special thanks to everyone on every branch of my family tree.

Very special thanks to my father, Manuel Dudum,
who would always recite *his* family tree to me...
Now I understand.

-RD

Text and illustrations copyright © 2023 by Richard M. Dudum

For information about permission to reproduce selections from this book:
Email: Richarddudum@gmail.com

Book design by Jodi McPhee

Published and illustrated: 2023

ISBN: 979-8-218-34256-2 (Hard cover)
ISBN: 979-8-218-40196-2 (Paperback)
ISBN: 979-8-218-34257-9 (eBook)

Printed in the U.S.A.

Elias Dudum
(great-great-grandfather)

Esa & Afifeh
(great-grandfather
and great-
grandmother)

Jirius & Sarah
(grandfather and
grandmother)

Isa. Dahir. Azizeh.
Manuel & Alice
(closest uncles, aunt,
and my parents)

Me
and mine!

Ramallah, Palestine

$\mathcal{A}$ long, long time ago,
long before me...

…my great-great-grandfather
planted my family tree.

At the end of his orange grove,
great-granddad would be…

...working and digging
while thinking of me.

The tree was small,
not much to see.
He sat, drank coffee,
and talked to my tree...

...telling stories and secrets
of days long gone by...
memories inside
of his mind's eye.

It's funny that he
would talk to a tree,
but he told stories to share
one day with me.

When he grew old,
    great-grandfather knew
he would never see
    his tree grow taller…
the tree he planted for me.

When I was a young boy,
  I met great-grandfather's tree,
now taller and stronger
  than I would ever be.

I reached for an orange
nearby me…

...remembering great-grandfather
and his days with my tree.

I would sit by my tree,
   where great-grandfather would be.
Rustling winds whispered
      his stories to me.

As I grew older,
   I began to see
things were changing
   around my family tree.

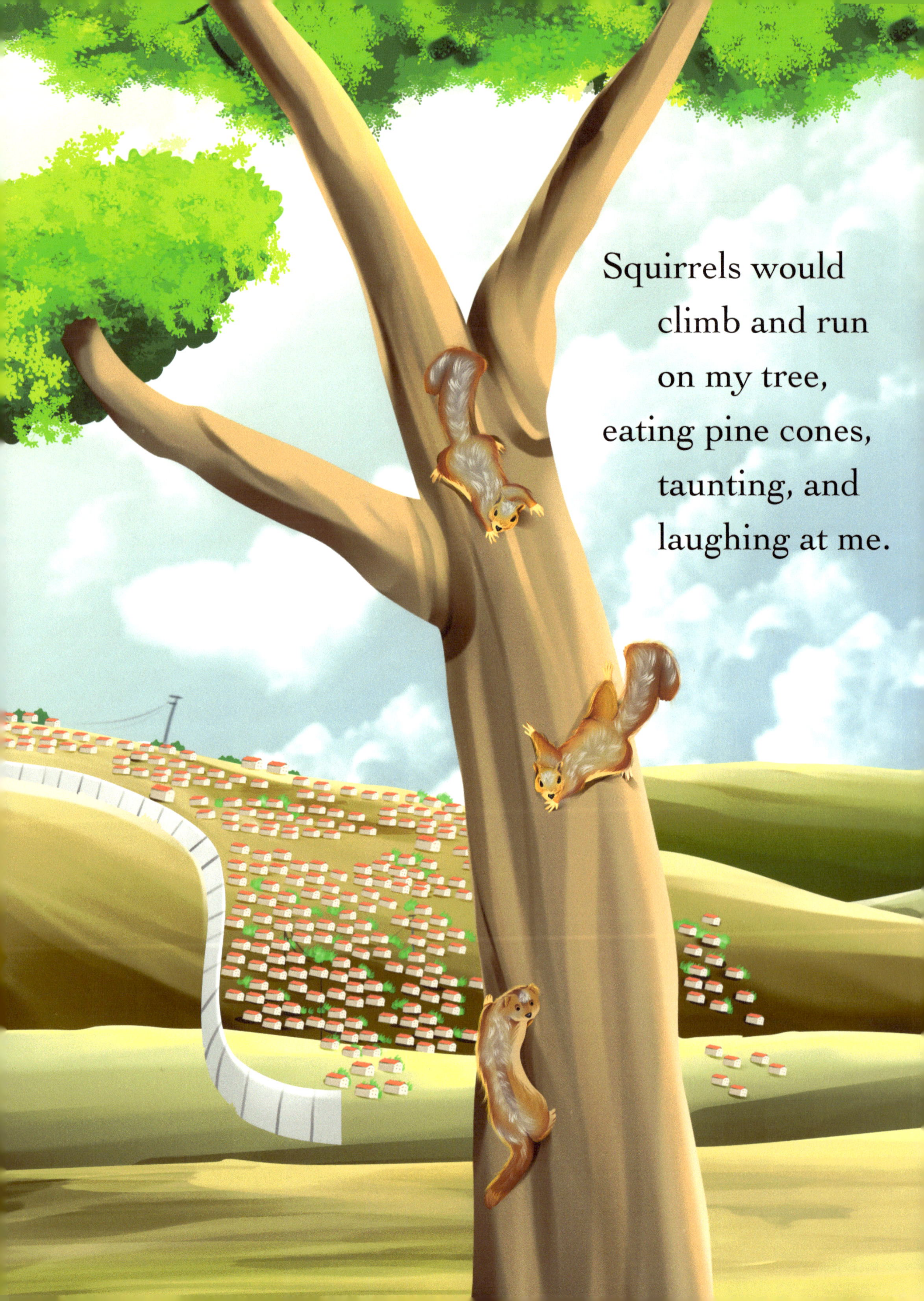

Squirrels would
climb and run
on my tree,
eating pine cones,
taunting, and
laughing at me.

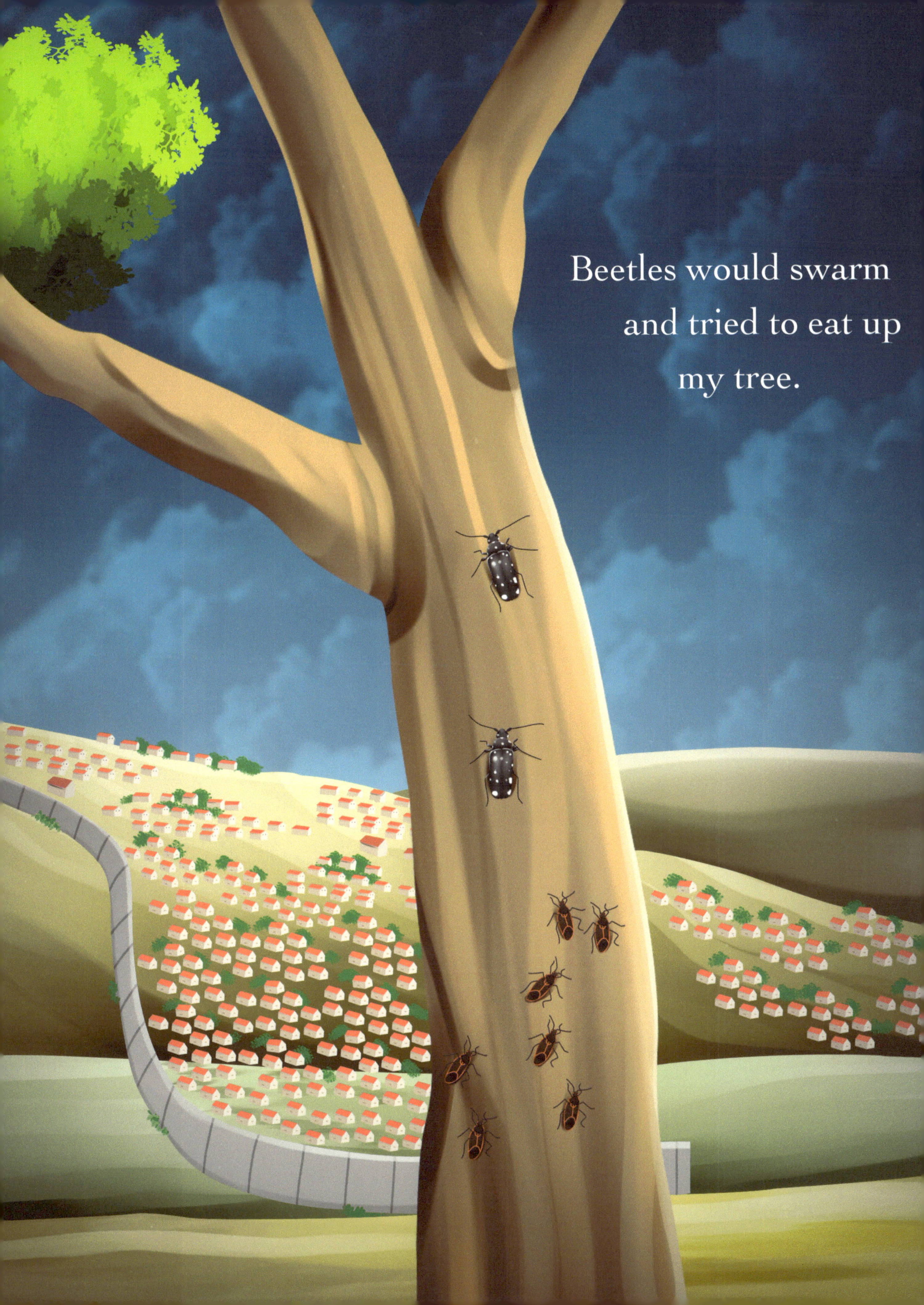

Beetles would swarm
and tried to eat up
my tree.

Raccoons would come
and sit in my tree,
breaking branches,
making messes,
and staring at me.

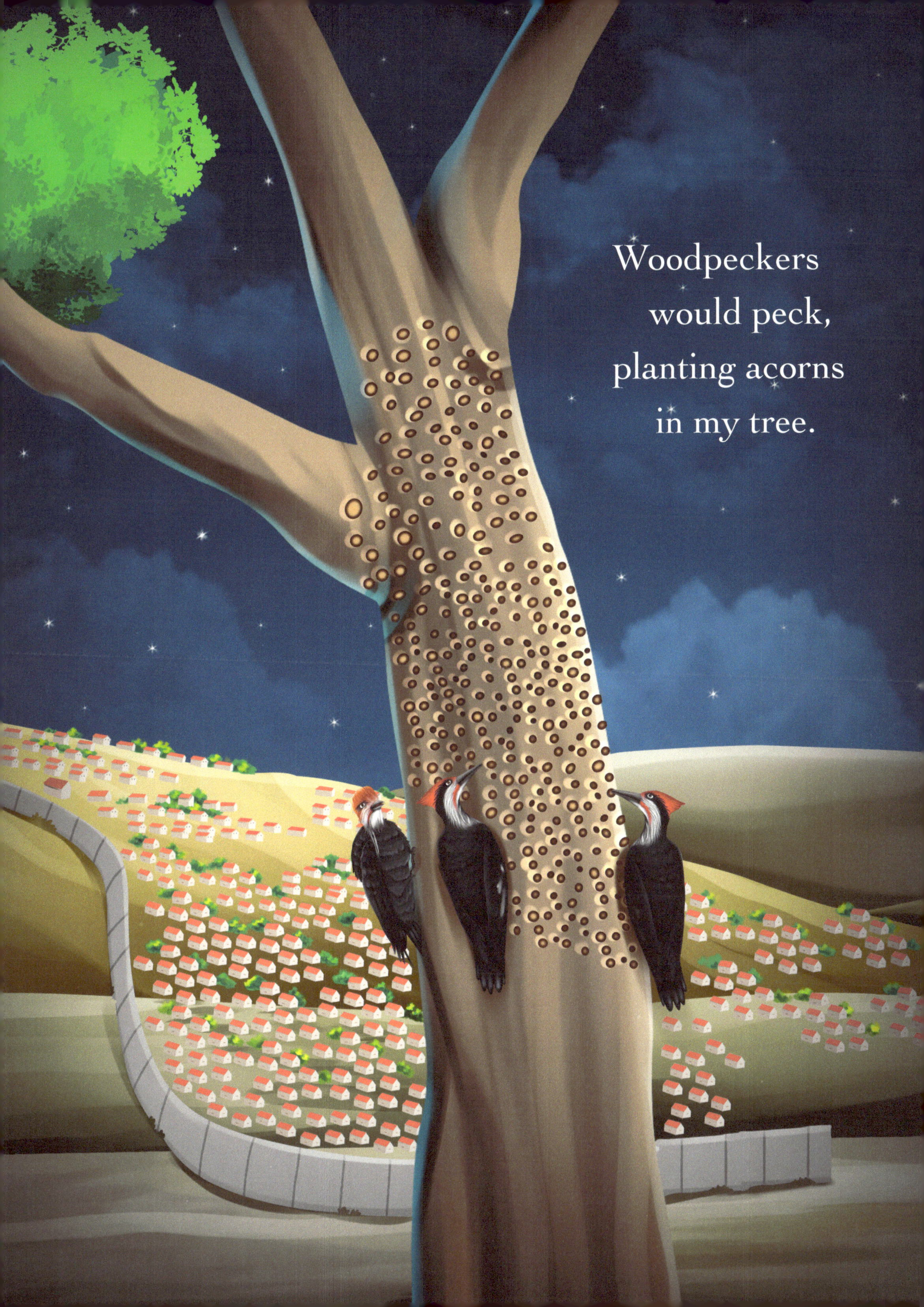

Woodpeckers
would peck,
planting acorns
in my tree.

I don't know why,
or how it could be...
so many pests
attacking my tree.

LOVE WINS

The wind even tried
to occupy my tree,
but my tree was too strong;
that will never be.

FREE
PALESTINE
= PEACE
= JUSTICE

THIS WALL WILL FALL

It seems to be,
    my tree, like me,
just wanted to be left alone,
    in peace and free.

And then one day,
it came to be.
I had to say goodbye
to great-grandfather's
tree.

My tree was old and tired, like me.
The tree was part of my family,
like great-grandfather
knew it would be.

I thought to myself,
  "How can this be?
My great-grandchildren will
    need their own family tree."

So we planted and nurtured
a strong little tree…

...that would last all their lifetimes, long after me.